What Do I Call My Love For Your Body?

JIDE BADMUS

First published in Great Britain
as a softback original in 2022

Copyright © Jide Badmus
The moral right of the author has been asserted.
All rights reserved.

No part of this publication may be reproduced, stored in a retrieval system, or transmitted, in any form or by any means, without the prior permission in writing of the author, nor be otherwise circulated in any form of binding or cover other than that in which it is published and without a similar condition including this condition being imposed on the subsequent purchaser.

Cover Design: Buzz Designz
Artwork: Martins Deep

Published by 'The Roaring Lion Newcastle'

Email: books@theroaringlionnewcastle.com

Website: www.theroaringlionnewcastle.com

ISBN: 978-1-913636-82-1
eISBN: 978-1-913636-83-8

OTHER BOOKS BY THE AUTHOR

- Obaluaye (FlowerSong Press, 2022)
- Scripture (Sevhage, 2018)
- There is a Storm in my Head (WRR, 2017)

Chapbooks

- Lust Alphabets (2022)
- Anatomy of the Sun (and everything underneath) (with Tukur Loba Ridwan) (2021)
- Silk Psalms (with Michael Alozor) (2021)
- Paradox of Little Fires (2021)
- Paper Planes in the Rain (with Pamilerin Jacob) (WRR, 2019)

Anthologies Curated & Edited by the Author

- How to Fall in Love (2020)
- Vowels Under Duress, An Anthology (2019)
- Coffee, An Anthology (2019)
- Today, I Choose Joy, An Anthology (2019)

*Lust is a lovely word and makes love
so much more interesting*

—Michael Faudet, *Lust*

Contents

PREFACE 1

YOUR BODY IS A POEM 3
    Body Language 4
    Your Body is a Poem 5
    Souvenir 6
    The Unveiling 7
    Pilgrimage 8
    This Way to Eden 9
    Knots 10
    The Shape of Us 11
    Orgasm 12
    Piggy Bank 13
    Skin 14
    Jacuzzi 15
    Torn 16
    Stutter 17
    Bandits 18

JAGUNLABI 19
    Rebel 20
    Riot 21
    Ashes 22
    Suicide Bomber 23
    Terrorist 24
    Frisk Me 25
    Warhead 26
    Gunnilingus 27
    Gunslinger 28
    Game of Thrones 29

Man of Steel 30
Iron Man 31
Blackout 32
Sweet Ruins 33
Night is a Battle Line 34

THE NATURE OF LUST 35
Weatherman... 36
First Day at Work After Honeymoon 37
Daffodils... 38
Rain 39
Precipitation 40
Monsoon 41
Horizon 42
Beach.. 43
Treasure Island 44
Camouflage 45
The Nature of Lust..................................... 46
The Nature of Man..................................... 47
The Rock 48
The Wedding Night 49
Daybreak 50

EXTENDED PLAY 51
Love Song... 52
Body of Music... 53
Extended Play 54
Fèrè 55
Lyrics 56
Soft Rock.. 57
Hard Rock 58
Duet.. 59

Craftsman 60
Jamming 61
Party By the Sea 62
A Journal of Eros 63
Basic INKstinct 64
Published 65
Orgy 66
WHAT DO I CALL MY LOVE FOR YOUR BODY? 67

ACKNOWLEDGEMENT 69
AUTHOR'S PROFILE 71

PREFACE

Love remains the most abused word—the most misused, the most inconsistent. It's a word with a million undertones and a complicated poise. Its innocence is that of a Reverend Father who has fathered a son. Its purity is that of rainwater gathered from rusty roofs.

What do I call my love for your body? Your Pastor would probably say it's the lust of the flesh. Your mother would probably agree. But lust is not a negative emotion—it's such a beautiful experience, a dark mystery begging for interrogation.

This collection of poems interrogates the body as a poem, as war, as nature's work of art, and, as music. A lover's body is a gift of love, a door to ecstasy—and so much more.

Jide Badmus
17th July, 2022

WHAT DO I CALL MY LOVE FOR YOUR BODY?

WHAT DO I CALL MY LOVE FOR YOUR BODY?

YOUR BODY IS A POEM

Body Language

My first lover told me
    the body is an expression
    —the human anatomy
    is a journal of emotions.
    She said the skin is full
    of mouths & taught me
    the vocabulary of flesh.
    She trained my eyes to
    speak in tongues of light,
    understand the different
    dialects of desire.

Your lips, at the edge of speech, part
        to reveal a fine diction of teeth.
        You roll back your tongue & hide
        the words in a brilliance of irises.
        Beneath a nuance of poise,
        a longing breathes under
        the pleats of your skirt.

WHAT DO I CALL MY LOVE FOR YOUR BODY?

Your Body is a Poem

Your body under that dress
is like seeds of thoughts
trapped in pods—like words
poised in shells, set to hatch
into beautiful lines of soft
curves, clefts, & contours.

Your eyes are as similes
for beauty & its synonyms.
Your lips are as enjambment
of smiles, a seductive opening
to the poem that is your body!

Without the encumbrances,
you reveal stark metaphors—
ripe agbalumo entreat to be
squeezed of their genius.

You have skin like sleek stanzas,
dimples as bold punctuations,
& a figure of sensual speeches.

Your body is a condensed
anthology, seducing eyes

with the nuances of nudity.

Souvenir

Your body is a metaphor
—a sea of light.
I walk into you, barefoot.
You welcome me with

a kiss, light on the lips,
& flip the switch.

You are a room
of laughter & sunshine.

My skin giggles at your touch.
You gift me live souvenirs—

a music of rain,
a dawning of wings,

& a breath of flora.

The Unveiling

Unzip amorous
portals of flesh.
Lure light—let it
into the secrets
of lacy lingerie.
I've seen your
body unveiled
severally
& each time
I am smitten
—eyes popping,
nerves standing
in veneration.

Pilgrimage

This body is
a blueprint to bliss—
a journey to *Jannah*!

Each time I traverse
her dark, sultry maze
I find new pieces of light,
treasures I must have
rushed past in the past!

Each time I run my hands
over this sensual sacrament,
I see the fourth man in the fire—
I be-come transfigured, a god
sipping on cocktails of worship!

My lover's body is
a map of freedom—
runway to Eden!

WHAT DO I CALL MY LOVE FOR YOUR BODY?

This Way to Eden

Dressed in nothing
but weaves & heels,
I stand, poised before you
as a street sign: *This way to Eden*
& set off frantic lights in your head.

I am as a crossroads—lips
& legs slightly parted,
hands perched on wide hips—
waiting on you to choose
the direction we're heading.

Imagine me as a zebra
crossing—here is safe,
bridge this space between us.
Fasten your lips on mine—
I can barely wait for your rugged palms.
Steer this eager body, clutch my breasts, &
cross into territories beneath my waistline
If you want to hear me rev!

Knots

She quivers like a feather
in the palms of the wind—
lips tremble like masts in
a storm of unspoken pleas.
Her skin aches, craves the
touch of a sensual quill...

My mouth slowly unwraps
the answer to her prayer—
greedy lips crash into a kiss
& dredge a crater of desire.
Palms roam carnal terrains
in search of pleasure spots—
plains, hills, & valleys...
An oasis of ecstasy!

Her body is a slave, loyal
to the rhythm of my touch.
I'm as grease to her gears!
We become a knot of urgency
& restraint—reckless & cautious—
we beat our bodies to the point
of satisfaction & total exhaustion!

The Shape of Us

Not quite like a trowel
turning soft, moist earth
—nor like the sun's teeth
ripping night's skin,
we knead each other
into passionate dough—
my loins yielding
to the yeast of your palms—
& pour ourselves into a mould
the shape of sex.

Orgasm

the plan is to get you out of this body
—place you on a sensual plane
& wear you sultry wings—
guide you through carnal terrains,
yet get you lost & craving
home—praying, stuttering,
spelling my name
in alien tongues...

WHAT DO I CALL MY LOVE FOR YOUR BODY?

Piggy Bank

The night is broke
but I come to you,
brimmed
—break me,
koló of emotions.
This stash of flesh
is all yours.

Skin

Èniyàn l'aṣọ—
how true this is
when we undress
only to wear
each other's
warm skins.

Jacuzzi

I am bare, safe for you
on my lean chest,

beaded whispers
& pendant smiles

cuddling me.
You probe

with antiseptic eyes,
bathe me in lithe light

—scrub the stress off my skin
with deft suppleness

& when I'm lathered up,
shower me with kisses

& wrap me in
a towel of flesh.

Torn

I need strength
to keep my body

from falling
helplessly for you.

I'm a city, torn.
My heart is

all over the place—
my head, on a mild restrain.

Stutter

I.
The heart can lie
but this body is drunk,

loose-tongued,
shamelessly honest
—it can't keep a secret.

II.
My bones creak
under the weight
of want. Lips flutter—
not for lack of courage
—the grammar of lust
is hard to master!

Nerves are upright,
limbs become liquid.
This emotion doesn't
falter—but the flesh,
it stutters...

III.
This longing may
not be coherent

as the beat of the heart
but it is sincere, a cock

at the hint of first light.
This skin has the conscience

of a gun, loyal to
your biddings.

Bandits

These feelings roam the streets of my body. This passion is prodigal, set to be squandered on you. I ache with an incomplete song. Your laughter is balm but the melody I seek is not the vocal honey springing from your tongue. I have the appetite of a flashlight biting into night's skin. My nerves scream with want like an ambulance in pursuit of healing—sirens blaring, blinkers pleading, reaching for you! These emotions are outlaws—bandits set to invade your soul, loot your flesh, & cart away your heart. These feelings roam the streets of my body, seeking a home in yours!

WHAT DO I CALL MY LOVE FOR YOUR BODY?

JAGUNLABI

Rebel

The cops patrolling the carnal borders
are either corrupt or complacent—
rebel desires have taken over this body!

Riot

I behold you
in your purest form
& my flesh becomes
a street under siege—
there is a riot in my loins.
Emotions are in pandemonium...
My body is a placard raised in protest—
touch me, hold me—calm this uprising!

Ashes

I crave your body
as cigarette covets fire.
I yearn for your breath on my flesh,
steak of desire on sensual grille.
Consume me from inside
like a dream, like steam
brewing in a kettle of lust.

Bare your weapons,
bring on this sultry war—
quell this unrelenting insurgence!
Invade this carnal fortress
until moans rise as white flags, &
smoke, above the ashes of ecstasy.

Suicide Bomber

I suspect she's here
with bad intentions
so, I strip her to reveal
secret sensual weaponry—
she's a bomb I must defuse!

Terrorist

Your body under that
dress is a time bomb.
Strip—initiate countdown.
Show me how you breached
this emotional fort, how you
escaped detection with this
artillery of chest—how you
took this embassy
of flesh hostage.

WHAT DO I CALL MY LOVE FOR YOUR BODY?

Frisk Me

Touch me...
touch me like you own me.
Frisk me—unearth hidden
passions. Frisk me (again)—
confiscate me like I'm a weapon.
Hold me, embrace me
as fire would fuel.
Empty me—fill me
with your whole.

Warhead

You wear light
on lithesome body—
full moons on chest.

But you stand before me
eaten half by shadows—
light hidden in dark lingerie.

I trace soft contours
with eyes, hands dying
to hold your trim waist
& taut butt, palms craving to feel
the moist sponge of your crotch,
lips brittle with want & tongue burned.

I feast on your lips
while frenzied fingers fumble
with zippers & buttons & hooks—
until soldier nipples leap out, combat ready,
& my warhead is raring to go.

We stroke ourselves with the fervour
of lawnmowers, purring, exploring
planets beneath our skins
till what is left of flesh are meteors—
till your scarlet blooms beg
for thrusts of rain...

Gunnilingus

push your *revulva* in my mouth—
I'll pull the trigger with my tongue
& make you die several times
in the arms of pleasure

Gunslinger

The streets are deserted.
Here we are, alone, two
gunslingers, poised lust-stark.
You have an advantage of hips
& bulletproof pubes. I die
by slugs from my own loins,
buried in your grave of flesh.

WHAT DO I CALL MY LOVE FOR YOUR BODY?

Game of Thrones

They say there can't be
two heads—only one heir
to the throne.

I say we can
reign together,
defy the norms.

I say we bare
natural artillery—
for there's no need
for a power tussle
in this *skindom.*

I say we start
with you above
& in charge of this
staff of authority,
grinding, gliding…

I say we switch
positions as we wish.
What only matters
is that I occupy
this Oval office.

They say there can't be
two heads. I say we show
them sixty-nine reasons
they can't be right!
On this throne, we
reign together.

WHAT DO I CALL MY LOVE FOR YOUR BODY?

Man of Steel

Don't! Don't touch
this dial that is me.

Tendrils of a smile.
Glints in your eyes.
This heart is stone dust.

How you make me
betray myself
with a kiss!

How you hold this
man of steel to your
mouth like a bullhorn charm!

Did I dissolve like
vanilla on your tongue?
Did I sing the secrets
I swore not to divulge?

How you beat me
into shape—how I am your
slave on this sensual anvil!

WHAT DO I CALL MY LOVE FOR YOUR BODY?

Iron Man

between a girl's thighs, a miry jaw
mouths a man into meekness

Blackout

Last night I walked through
your body, lighting up the streets
with fireworks like it was a carnival.

Then your city came under siege—
sensual walls broken down.
We took refuge in burning cathedrals

Last night we wore skins of war.
Fighter jets roared in our heads.
You said a prayer & held onto me...

This morning you asked me
how we survived last night—
Baby, I died...where the hell are we?

WHAT DO I CALL MY LOVE FOR YOUR BODY?

Sweet Ruins

You left these here:
sweet sores like tyre tracks on coal tar,
scars of a stream from where we drank last night.

These here are the aftermath of an earthquake:
a broken strap of bra, a fallen earring,
& the shadow of your scent.

These here are the spoils of war:
scratch &bite marks, the vestige of kisses,
& a flame that is eager to dance again!

WHAT DO I CALL MY LOVE FOR YOUR BODY?

Night is a Battle Line

Come to war stark.
Blend with night in
supple camouflage.

Bare, you are
an artillery
—laced arrows

on a bow of bust.
Fold your skin,
go to work—

forge my body
into a weapon.
Fashion this flesh

into a sultry blade.
Mould desire
into silk bullets.

Two grenades
dangle between
my legs—

pull out passion's pin with
mouth—watch me shatter
into delightful shrapnel.

WHAT DO I CALL MY LOVE FOR YOUR BODY?

THE NATURE OF LUST

Weatherman

Is it not beautiful
that you could always tell when
my dawn is pregnant with a storm?
You spread like an umbrella
to meet the morning rain.

First Day at Work After Honeymoon

It rained all morning—and all afternoon. The thoughts of you wouldn't let me attend to the mob on my desk—the thoughts of weather wasting away...Evening came, shaped as a salvation for burdened bodies, lovers sphered by infinite desires. You were on my favourite couch, caramel skin wrapped in silk, when I came home. Bodies under duress screamed for hands and lips. And tongues. The rain resumed singing—my fire danced on your waters. And we thundered into ashes and embers.

Daffodils

the way you pluck me
out of this pair of briefs
reminds me of a field
of yellow flowers.
You hold me
softly by the stalk &
plant me between lips—
it's Spring in your mouth
& I bloom into a geyser
of nectar.

Rain

embrace me
seep into me
like rain

touch me with fluid palms
make emotions sprout
like flowers from this bed

kiss me
please me in torrents
pour the whole of you into me

Precipitation

When our lips lock,
we become as master
key to a world of bliss.

Bodies take the form of
knives & whetstones—
gliding, grinding, defying friction.

Our needs intersect as lust-laden
Winds. The sky opens & we thunder
into perspiration.

Monsoon

I come, monsoon, into your city—
hands, as feet, crossing borders—
exploring terrains under your blouse.
Tongues crash into each other like waves
& lips drown in tides of kisses as fingers
rustle seaweeds at your shoreline
with prophecies of the coming storm.

Horizon

a canoe on her high sea,
my paddle stabs into ardent tides
aiming for the horizon.
Empty seashells, we lie
on an ethereal shore where
earth touches heaven—
there is calm & we hold on
to the vestiges of a terrific tempest.

WHAT DO I CALL MY LOVE FOR YOUR BODY?

Beach

Sunny eyes,
summer lips—
serve me a cocktail
of light & warmth.

Sandy skin pleads for footprints.
Petals encumbered pray for feet
of seas & voice of waves.
It's a season of moulting—
shed this bikini, let me
bless your body with a tan!

Treasure Island

Let's say I'm a rock. Your
windy hands lunge at me,
sweep off top soil,
leave me bare &
barely breathing.
Let's say I'm a house
on the rock—
you're a force
I can't withstand.
The storm will come,
shatter windows of longing,
barge through walls, doors.
Lightning will blind me.
Thunder, grind me into
fine grains, dust of passion.
I'm a leaking ceiling,
the floor is flooding.
You offer a life jacket of lips,
yacht of warm skin—and
an island to hide my head.

Camouflage

My lover's body
is a beautiful disaster—
yesterday she was volcano,
today, a tsunami...who knows
what form the storm will take
tomorrow?

WHAT DO I CALL MY LOVE FOR YOUR BODY?

The Nature of Lust

I.

Let your lips of dew open my bud to light.
Breathe on these petals like morning rays.
Kiss my pollen, sweet butterfly.

II.

Pluck me out of these clouds—
wear the voice of waterfall &
drum loving gibberish to my ears.

Make your touch soft as feathers—
glide over my skin like a river, purring,
stroking earth with soothing palms.

III.

I will respond to the thunder of your thrusts
with a cooing of my own—a gratitude of
moans.
We'll become as victims of an earthquake in
the arms of ecstasy

The Nature of Man

I dissolve.
Lumps of jazz—vibes
in ambient horizons.
Desire dusks here,
stripper butterflies
dripping nectar & stars
in the eyes of night.

I open up.
Soft petals
in the palm
of moaning dews
—sun, eager to breathe.
I lurk in the ribs of your garden.

The Rock

Your touch stirs
the dragon in me.
Your soft skin awakens
the volcano in my veins
from dormancy—the rock
in my crotch is about to explode!

The Wedding Night

Dawn is a marriage
between night & day—
an intersection of light
& shadows as beautiful
as a wedding ceremony
or a first shared orgasm.

Daybreak

day broke
on your face

I flicked moon crumbs
off your eyebrows

& watched your pupils
dew honey & malt

dawn yawned &
raven desires

cawed at a distance.
Something is birthed

in me. A blessing.
But every blessing comes

with a curse, an emptiness,
a pang of lust—

the appetite of mists,
the thirst of waterfalls,

the longing of chaste
wings for ovulating skies.

Come, ease into me,
breakfast of sunlight,

fill my morning
with your grace.

WHAT DO I CALL MY LOVE FOR YOUR BODY?

EXTENDED PLAY

Love Song

You pluck my strings,
you play a melodious tune,
but I can't dance
until your back finds
the ache in my bed.
Your fingers play
an ethereal symphony.
You tongue turns
parched lawns green.
I just want to lie here,
watch the sun rise with you
—I just want to keep this
beautiful song on replay.

Body of Music

bare bodies
naked notes
singing skins
lust lyrics
restless rhythm
lilt in my loins

Extended Play

the air is awkward
a gulf waits to be
filled with music

a cappella
of wine glasses
becomes instrumental
to what comes next

aching cymbals of lips
eager plectrum, restless strings
—passion's coal is seething red

momentum breaks
speed limit
there's a prodding,
a yielding—
my poem forms
on your gaping page

the bed sings
an orchestra,
a falsetto of moans

Fèrè

With my mouth on your organ
& yours around my flute, we begin
This orchestra—grunting in falsettos—
Blending baritone moans & timbre tones
In a crescendo of exclamations.

Lyrics

There's a tune I want to play:
Flute of lips & cymbals of
Breasts—drum on bums &
Chew on lyrics yet *unmastered*.

WHAT DO I CALL MY LOVE FOR YOUR BODY?

Soft Rock

Your soft lips find
   rhythm in mine.
   There's a chorus
   of swelling, ad lib
   on nipples
   —rippling skins
   vibrating veins
   & a percussion
   of flesh.

Hard Rock

    desire holds night
by the throat, thrums softly
to whispers of falling silk
then enters a nubile verse,
wild cymbals breathing fast,
clanging, banging—
lithe bodies writhe
to the voice of fire...

Duet

The dawn hatches a song.
Alto desires climb out of bed.

Pious hymns rise in penile throat,
a chorus of wings beneath my fly.

Our hearts stop to beat—
a cappella of longing breaths,

a refrain of bodies undressing,
trembling lips, throbbing veins.

We fumble through notes
of flesh in search of key,

in search of fitting lyrics...
in search of rapture.

Craftsman

Urge me. Forge me.
Blend me into a song—
make me answer to the
voice of your hands.

WHAT DO I CALL MY LOVE FOR YOUR BODY?

Jamming

I hear the music
of your yearnings,

symphonies clawing
through dark clefts,

velvet folds, &
verdant, psalms-dripping skin.

I feel keen voices
throbbing in my veins,

telling me that I am robust,
brimmed with warm songs

for you. You become
lust instrument in my hands,

solfa in my bones...
I hold you in my palms

—twerking *sekere*—
& play you on baritone prick.

Party By the Sea

Fire dances to the sea's samba.
The night sweats. The moon
& stars turn fugitives
on the eve of ecstasy.
What is left of the bonfire
is a coven of smoke
—sated shells
on a shore of ashes

A Journal of Eros

verse waits
to be written on

the page of night. You open,
lust bud, into pliant petals.

I come as erotic dew,
moist metaphors, lush chorus...

I reword you, manuscript—
willing clay, supple to touch.

I knead abstractions into form.
Into light. We come together,

rhyming lips, enjambed loins
—a journal of gasps & grunts.

Basic INKstinct

I write of secret places, hidden
treasures & sacred pleasures—

tales of ripples, storms
& flaming passions.

I write of stolen kisses, covert fires
& sacral juices—memoirs of locked

doors, unbridled moans
& rumpled sheets.

I write of a drowning, a rising
& a blooming horizon

—songs of breasts,
clefts, & ecstasy.

WHAT DO I CALL MY LOVE FOR YOUR BODY?

Published

"...this book
of ache and longing..."
—K. Y Robinson

Come, succumb to
your nagging heart,
fill the pages of night
with the alphabets
of our deepest yearnings.

Write the lurid scenes
in your head on my skin.
Speak of the tinglings,
the swellings,
the numbness—
errant sensations,
wilding between
attrition & tenderness.

Let's edit the world
into temporal inexistence
—fill the air with paragraphs
of pleas & moans & giggles.
Let's publish this love—this
poetry of hearts & loins is due
a space on the shelf of ecstasy.

Orgy

When sleep eludes, thoughts
      Lie on my mental bed,
      Naked virgins about to
      Taste forbidden bread...
      Imagination is a square moon.
      Beneath its glare, keen words
      Flourish in an orgy.

WHAT DO I CALL MY LOVE FOR YOUR BODY?

You sound like a child,
yet to grasp the concept
of relationships—she asks
Daddy, are you my friend?

Your words stood on a leg
like a cock on foreign land.
Your soft voice shook the earth—
Do you love me? You asked
after I'd just served you
a dinner of myself.

I wanted to scream at you,
tell you I love you—but how do I
make you understand that
love has a spectrum of meanings?

Yes, I love you—or what else
do I call my love for your body?

WHAT DO I CALL MY LOVE FOR YOUR BODY?

ACKNOWLEDGEMENT

"Blackout" was first published in 2020 by Perhappened Magazine.

"day break" was first published in 2022 by Discretionary Love.

WHAT DO I CALL MY LOVE FOR YOUR BODY?

AUTHOR'S PROFILE

Jide Badmus is an engineer, a poet inspired by beauty and destruction. He believes that things in ruins were once beautiful.

He is the author of There is a Storm in my Head; Scripture; Paper Planes in the Rain; Paradox of Little Fires; Silk Psalms; Anatomy of the Sun (and everything beneath); Lust Alphabets; and Obaluaye (FlowerSong Press, 2022). He was nominated for a Pushcart Prize in 2021.

Badmus has curated/edited anthologies such as Vowels Under Duress; Coffee; Today, I Choose Joy; and How to Fall in Love.

WHAT DO I CALL MY LOVE FOR YOUR BODY?

He is founder of INKspiredNG, the Poetry Editor for Con-scio Magazine, and sits on the board of advisors for Libretto Magazine.

Jide is married, with two daughters. He writes from Lagos, Nigeria and tweets @bardmus

WHAT DO I CALL MY LOVE FOR YOUR BODY?

Printed in Dunstable, United Kingdom